THE GREATEST SHOWMAN

T0081636

Audio Arrangements by Peter Deneff

To access audio visit:
www.halleonard.com/mylibrary

Enter Code
4573-2327-9217-3874

ISBN 978-1-5400-2848-8

7777 W. BLUEMOUND RD. P.O. BOX 13819 MILWAUKEE, WI 53213

In Australia Contact:
Hal Leonard Australia Pty. Ltd.
4 Lentara Court
Cheltenham, Victoria, 3192 Australia
Email: ausadmin@halleonard.com.au

Visit Hal Leonard Online at
www.halleonard.com

COME ALIVE

VIOLA

Words and Music by BENJ PASEK
and JUSTIN PAUL

FROM NOW ON

VIOLA

Words and Music by BENJ PASEK
and JUSTIN PAUL

THE GREATEST SHOW

VIOLA

Words and Music by BENJ PASEK,
JUSTIN PAUL and RYAN LEWIS

A MILLION DREAMS

VIOLA

Words and Music by BENJ PASEK
and JUSTIN PAUL

NEVER ENOUGH

VIOLA

Words and Music by BENJ PASEK
and JUSTIN PAUL

THE OTHER SIDE

VIOLA

Words and Music by BENJ PASEK
and JUSTIN PAUL

REWRITE THE STARS

VIOLA

Words and Music by BENJ PASEK
and JUSTIN PAUL

THIS IS ME

VIOLA

Words and Music by BENJ PASEK
and JUSTIN PAUL

TIGHTROPE

VIOLA

Words and Music by BENJ PASEK
and JUSTIN PAUL